Reading Article 15 and *Manusmriti.*

Open Windows: A Feminist Research Center.

This is a collaboration of Lies and Big Feet;
an independent publishing house.

ISBN: 9384281131
ISBN-13: 978-9384281137

What we consider as infallible, sacred religious texts which comprise of "revealed knowledge" is actually a compilation of many texts and changes must have occurred in them through centuries, as they were handed down through generations.

CONTENTS

Introduction.

ARTICLE 15 OF THE CONSTITUION OF INDIA

It is one thing when religious institutions talk about God and the Supreme Being and the Hindu *shastras,* and it is also another thing when these institutions also throw in a lot of theology which is outright misogynous and sexist and caste-ist, and thereby exclude half the population of India. Are religious institutions participants in propounding sexist and caste-ist theology which affects how people engage in their every-day lives? Do these institutions therefore, violate the Fundamental Rights that are granted to all the citizens of India by the Constitution?

If caste-ist and sex-ist discourse is allowed to function in the public realm, it tantamounts to being unconstitutional and comprises a violation of one of the Fundamental Rights that has been granted in India, namely, Article15 of the Constitution of India and is the Right to Equality.

15. Prohibition of discrimination on grounds of religion, race, caste, sex or place of birth.-

(1) The State shall not discriminate against any citizen on grounds only of religion, race, caste, sex, place of birth or any of them.

(2) No citizen shall, on grounds only of religion, race, caste, sex, place of birth or any of them, be subject to any disability, liability, restriction or condition with regard to-

(a) access to shops, public restaurants, hotels and places of public entertainment;

(b) the use of wells, tanks, bathing ghats, roads and places of public resort maintained wholly or partly out of State funds or dedicated to the use of the general public.

(3) Nothing in this article shall prevent the State from making any special provision for women and children.

1[(4) Nothing in this article or in clause (2) of article 29 shall prevent the State from making any special provision for the advancement of any socially and educationally backward classes of citizens or for the Scheduled Castes and the Scheduled Tribes.]

2[(5) Nothing in this article or in sub-clause (g) of clause (1) of article 19 shall prevent the State from making any special provision, by law, for the advancement of any socially and educationally

backward classes of citizens or for the Scheduled
Castes or the Scheduled Tribes in so far as such
special provisions relate to their admission to
educational institutions including private educational
institutions, whether aided or unaided by the State,
other than the minority educational institutions
referred to in clause (1) of article 30.]

The fact that religious institutions often and always
propagate misogyny ridden social dictums and equate them
with notions of Existence and Hindu theology, makes us
question the constitutional validity of the practise, as it is a
flagrant violation of Article 15, which aims towards
undoing all discriminatory practises.

The larger question which we should all strive towards is:
why should the Hindu *shastras* be seen as comprising, in its
totality, "revealed knowledge" when large chunks of it refer
to temporal behavior that is based on one's gender or caste
(the most oft-cited being *Manusmriti's Varnashrama*). Why
are they cited as being infallible when often these texts
propound extremely sexist and caste-ist views?[1]

---

[1] Throughout, I will be referring to *Manusmriti* and *Manavadharma*,
synonymously. I will be using the following text: *Manavadharmasastra, or, The
Institutes of Manu*, according to the Gloss of Kulluka, comprising the Indian
system of Duties, Religious and Civil. Verbally translated from the original,
with a Preface by Sir William Jones, and Collated with the Sanskrit Text, by
Graves Chanmey Haughton, Esq., Professor of Hindu Literature in the
East India College. THIRD EDITION, edited by The Revd. P. Percival,
Professor of Vernacular Literature, Presidency College, Madras. (Madras,J.

The yet unresolved conundrum, thus is: how does the Indian state (which is also a signatory to CEDAW) allow these texts to be a part of public discourse as they are often, and mostly, quite unconstitutional? The rampant sexist and caste-ist discourse that is intrinsic to our Hindu *shastras* is overt and unapologetic.

How we, that is, women – eat, breathe, dress and conduct ourselves and the kinds of labor that we are allowed to perform – are codified and seen as intrinsic to the Hindu *shastras*. The realm of religion, indeed, is the privilege of men. And indeed, it would not be salacious to argue that self-identifying Brahmin men and those who function in the religious institutions and are the so-called custodians of Hindu *dharma* are mostly myopic; they are unable to distinguish between what constitutes "revealed knowledge" about Existence and Brahman and Creation, and temporal gender-caste based social modes of being. What prevents the government of India (which is also a signatory to CEDAW) from slapping legal cases against these religious institutions as they propound unconstitutional rhetoric that, in all respects, violates our Fundamental Rights that are embedded within the Indian Constitution?

Higginbotham: 1863).

The larger question, though, is: can we ever take it for a given that what we know, in a definitive manner, as being central to the Hindu *shastras* can be construed as being infallible? - for all we know – these texts might have been amended and changes made as they were handed down generations. In the preface to his version of *Manavadharma*, Sir William Jones wrote about the textual variations that existed and how he collated different versions that were available in manuscript form to arrive at his final text:[2]

> At length appeared KULLU'KA BHATTA; who, after a painful course of study and the collation of numerous manuscripts, produced a work, of which it may, perhaps, be said very truly, that it is the shortest, yet the most luminous, the least ostentatious, yet the most learned, the deepest, yet the most agreeable, commentary ever composed on any author [namely, Manu] ancient or modern, European or Asiatic. The Pandits care so little for genuine chronology, that none of them can tell me the age of KULLU'KA, whom they always name with applause; but he informs us himself, that he was a *Brahmin* of the *Varéndra* tribe, whose family had been long settled in *Gaur* or Bengal, but that he had chosen his residence among the learned on the banks of the holy river at Ka'si. His text and interpretation I have almost implicitly followed,

2 Ibid.

though I had myself collated many copies of
MANU, and among them a manuscript of a very
ancient date: ...

We can arrive at the obvious conclusion that William Jones
consulted many textual variations of the *Manusmriti*, and if
so, the implication is that there was no single authoritative
text. If these texts that constitute our Hindu *shastras* are
unreliable with numerous variants existing simultaneously,
then it stands to reason that there is no authentic version
that we can refer to as being the original. Who is to tell as
to which part comprised "revealed knowledge" and which
sections were subsequent add-ons?

Open Windows: A Feminist Research Center.

1 THE UNSTABLE SACRED TEXT.

Manuscripts of the Hindu religious texts were often transferred onto print in the early years of print culture in colonial Bengal, India, (i.e. during the last decades of the eighteenth century) under the aegis of the East India Company sponsored Orientalists, but what exactly were the processes involved? How did native-brahmins look upon it as they assisted the Britishers in making the shift take place from a manuscript culture to a realm of print technology?

In 1825, Graves Chamney Haughton, a professor of Hindu Literature in the East India College, published an out-of-print text, William Jones's translation of the Sanskrit *Manava Dharma Shastra* or the *Institutes of Manu*.[3] Haughton's prefatory note states that it was a new edition of Sir William Jones's translation; he writes that in his own text "the version of the learned translator has been carefully

---

[3] Ibid.

revised and compared" and that discrepancies would have been a result of the "variety of the manuscripts consulted by Sir William Jones." This observation provides us with historical documentation that there existed a "variety" of manuscripts that were consulted by these Orientalist scholars as they wrote their versions of the *Manusmriti*.

In 1794, the British government of India had Jones's *Manava Dharma* printed; Sir William Jones, writes in his preface about the processes involved in collaborating with the Brahmins in writing the text:

> …[A]nd the brahman, who read it with me, requested most earnestly, that his name might be concealed; nor would he have read it for any consideration on a forbidden day of the moon,… so great, indeed, is the idea of sanctity annexed to this book, that, when the chief magistrate at Benaras endeavoured, at my request, to procure a Persian translation of it, before I had a hope of being at any time able to understand the original, the Pandits of his court unanimously and positively refused to assist in the work; nor should I have procured it at all, if a wealthy Hindu at Gaya had not caused the version to be made by some of his dependants."

The question to ask is thus: did natives operate within a different parallel epistemic world where multiple manuscripts of the same text were seen as legitimate; moreover, why were the brahmins not necessarily keen to see their names on print, but neither were they hesitant to transfer a manuscript culture onto print? These early decades of colonial print can throw more light on the nature of religious-manuscripts that existed in India, before the advent of print in India. More importantly and is of relevance, is that: when we read a text like *Manusmriti*, why exactly should we assume that there exists an intact, untouched, version of the text?

Till as recently as two hundred years ago, India was a manuscript culture meaning that the printed text did not exist. When the transition took place from a manuscript culture to a print one, it seems to have taken place easelessly, implying that the shift was made without much murmurs and complaints from at least the native, elite sections of society. The Britishers, on the other hand, at seeing the beautiful manuscripts in Indian languages, must have been reminded of their pre-print past and a lot of care was taken to ensure that these manuscripts were well kept. When Tipu Sultan lost the Mysore wars (1780-90s), his library was also taken and a concern was raised by the Company soldiers as to how the manuscripts were to be kept safe: "That part of the library of the late Tippoo Sultan, which was presented by the army to the Court of Directors, is lately arrived in Bengal; the Governor-General strongly recommends that the Oriental manuscripts composing this collection, should be deposited in the library of the College of Fort William, and it is his intention to retain the manuscripts accordingly, until he shall receive the orders of the Court upon the subject."[4] There was no rampant erasure of the Indian manuscript past, and in fact, the Company was keen to preserve this aspect of Indian culture.

———————————————————————————

Sir William Jones, referred to as the father of scientific linguistics and comparative philology, is a perfect example of a scholar who worked outside the Orientalist knowledge-making framework. He was also steeped in the culture of eighteenth century British print and had an immense trust in the veracity of printed texts. By the time of Sir William Jones, England had become an increasingly print-oriented society, shifting away from its oral past. This explains Jones' feverish desire to transcribe every manuscript into print, as the process would lend an element of fixity to unstable scribal texts. In an advertisement in *The Calcutta Gazette*, in 1789, Sir William Jones wrote:

The correctness of modern Arabian and

---

[4] *The Annals of the College of Fort William, from the Period of its Foundation.*Arranged and Published by Thomas Roebuck, Calcutta, Printed by Philip Periera at the Hindoostanee Press, 1819. "Introduction" pp. xxv. The report mentions the importance of preserving old manuscripts: "The preservation and augmentation of the Collection of Eastern Manuscripts, afford the only means of arresting the progressive destruction of Oriental learning. Since the dismemberment of the Muslim, those works have been dispersed over India, and have been exposed to the injuries and hazards of time, accident and neglect. It is worthy of the ambition of this great Empire to employ every effort of its influence in preserving from destruction and decay, these valuable records of Oriental history, Science and Religion." p. 114.

Persian Books is truly deplorable, nothing can
preserve them in any degree of accuracy but
the art of printing; and if Asiatic literature
should ever be general, it must diffuse itself,
as Greek learning was diffused in Italy after
the taking of Constantinople, by mere
impressions of the best manuscripts without
versions or comments, which future scholars
would add at their leisure to future editions:
but no printer should engage in so expensive a
business without the patronage and the purse
of monarchs of states, or society of wealthy
individuals or at least without a large public
subscription.[5]

Jones was extremely conscious of entering a realm of
scribal culture in Bengal, and this is reflected in his desire
to constantly transfer manuscripts into printed texts. In a
way, by transferring written texts into print, his central aim
was to codify knowledge, and in the process allow for
control of what was disseminated about India.[6] In 1768,
before Jones sailed for India, he wrote to Count Revicski,
the Imperial Minister of Warsaw, describing the difficulties
that were present when trying to locate a single meaning in
manuscripts; it was "impossible to find two manuscripts [of
Oriental literature] without error," he wrote, and "it was

---

[5] William Jones, *The Calcutta Gazette*, October 29, 1789.

[6] William Jones, *The Collected Works of Sir William Jones. 3 Vols.* (New York:
New York University Press, 1993), *Vol. 3*, p. 34.

"absolutely necessary … to possess two copies of every one" which he would read so that "faults of the one" would be "corrected by the other."[7] In many of his letters, Jones voices a similar concern, where he reveals an intense desire to transcribe everything that he reads into print. Writing to one Dr. Patrick Russel in 1786, he said, "I congratulate you on the completion of your two works, but exhort you to publish them."[8] Jones goes on to say, "think how much fame Koenig lost by delaying his publications" and even if printing is "dear at Calcutta," if "government" printed Russel's works, he would "cheerfully superintend commas and colons."[9] A year later, Jones voices a similar concern in another letter,

> I have just read a very old book on that art [of music] in Sanskrit. I hope to present the world with the substance of it, as soon as the transactions of our society [The Asiatic Society] can be printed; but we go slowly, since the press is often engaged by government; … The *Asiatik Miscellany*, to which you allude, is not the publication of our society, who mean to print no scraps, nor any *mere* translations. It was the undertaking of a private gentleman, and will certainly be of use in diffusing Oriental literature, though it has [not?] been so correctly printed as I

---

[7] Jones, *Complete Works, Vol. 1*, p. 101.

[8] Jones, *Complete Works, Vol. 2*, p. 99.

[9] Ibid., pp. 100-101.

could wish.[10]

Manuscripts are seen as being less than perfect while printed texts allow for true, correct knowledge to emerge. Print technology is invested with a kind of truth power that is denied to manuscripts. Power resides in the capacity to be able to use print, and in the process, to make it accessible to larger groups of people. Mechanical reproducibility, made possible as a result of letterpress technology, would make knowledge more reproducible but also more authentic. The realm of print spread across continents, and made it possible to control the colonial territories.

---

[10] Ibid., pp. 123-124.

2 THE SHIFT FROM A PRE-MODERN MANUSCRIPT CULTURE TO A REALM OF PRINT MODERNTIY.

Empire making was made possible through the realm of print culture. Not only was the technology transferred, but so were the socially ascribed characteristics of print. Sir William Jones, operating within the ideology of eighteenth century print culture that associated print with truth, assumed that the technology of print had the power to transform a pre-modern, Indian scribal culture into western modernity. But this equation between print and truth was not intrinsic to letterpress technology as till the early decades of the eighteenth century, in Europe, there was a suspicion of the printed word. In *The Nature of the Book: Print and Knowledge in the Making*, Adrian Johns draws attention to assumptions about print culture, stating that what we "often regard as essential elements and necessary concomitants of print are in fact rather more contingent than generally acknowledged. Veracity in particular is … extrinsic to the press itself, and has had to be grafted onto it."[11] A printed book could never be trusted to be what it claimed. Johns claims that in the seventeenth century, piracy and plagiarism were dominant fears. It was a matter of routine that books could be considered dubious; therefore, it was impossible to trust any printed report. Pirate editions of Shakespeare, Donne and Sir Thomas Browne were liable to egregious errors, and so was Sir Isaac Newton's unauthorized publication of *Principia* and the first scientific journal, the *Philosophical Transactions*. It was only in 1760 that the first book was printed without any errors.

There is nothing intrinsic to print for the technology to be considered as masculine and rational in comparison to manuscript texts. The characteristics of masculinity were socially ascribed to printed texts. In the early modern period in England, for example, writers were hesitant to see their works being printed, or to be seen ideologically and physically as involved in the marketplace of printers and publication. For the female writer, Jody Greene argues, publication was akin to prostitution, while the male writers shared this anxiety more acutely.[12] The act of publication, that is, submitting one's works to the press, made the writer vulnerable to charges of sexual deviance and indecent exposure. "The male writer," according to Wendy Wall, "always trades on his vulnerability when he agrees to play

---

[11] Adrian Johns, *The Nature of the Book: Print and Knowledge in the Making* (Chicago: University of Chicago Press, 2000), p. 2.

[12] Jody Greene, "Francis Kirkman's Counterfeit Authority: Autobiography, Subjectivity, Print," *PMLA* 121(1): 17-32.

the female role and be 'pressed' for the public."[13] By the seventeenth century, in England, increased literacy, the growth of cities and the flow of international capital improved print technology, and authors were more willing to make public works that would have a century ago been limited to private consumption. This caused an explosion in the number of printed books, doing away with how print was conceived. In eighteenth century England, print was seen at the apex of the communication system. And this was the nature of imperial print technology that was transferred to India, under the rule of the East India company; print was imbued with all the characteristics of the British nation and construed as vigorous, rational and truthful in comparison to an pre-modern, manuscript culture in India.

Nathaniel Halhed's *A Grammar of the Bengal Language*[14] was printed in 1778, and was one of the first printed texts in India. It had a multilingual title page; it had a Bengali subtitle alongside the English title (and the Roman numericals at the bottom), making it undoubtedly a first of its kind. Halhed has to be seen as working within the existing ideological notions of empire making, where Britain defined itself as civilized and modern by

---

[13] Wendy Wall, *The Imprint of Gender: Authority and Publication in the English Renaissance* (Ithaca, Cornell UP, 1993), p. 182.

[14] Nathaniel Halhed, *A Grammar of the Bengal Language*, 1778. Reprint, ed. R. C. Alston (England: The Scolar Press, 1969).

characterizing India and its languages as primitive. The author draws attention to the mechanical aspects of print technology; the natives are emasculated and deviant, awaiting British colonization for progress, and in a similar manner, archaic Indian scribal culture would undergo modern change through print technology. In order to maintain order and control the colonies, it was essential to learn the languages of the Indians—the underlying assumption was that the territorial domain of the colonies could be managed through the realm of print.

Halhed's grammar book has reasons to be lauded as the first in many ways: most importantly, it was multilingual, involving the efforts of both the English and the natives. For the natives, living within a manuscript culture, to see printed texts emerge, transcribing and documenting Bengali words and their English synonyms, would have been a unique experience. The book was printed in Hooghly, made its way to England and was sold in London by Elmsley. In 1783, a review in an English journal, *The English Review*, succinctly pointed to the numerous aspects of ingenuity in the book:[15]

> The work now before us (the first perhaps printed in Hindostan) has many circumstances of novelty, as well as of utility to recommend it to public attention. One gentleman presents us with the elements of a

---

[15] Review of "A Grammar of the Bengal Language," *The English Review, or, An Abstract of English and Foreign Literature* Vol. I (1783): 5-14.

language hitherto disregarded, and almost unknown in Europe. Another gentleman employs the extraordinary efforts of a singular and persevering genius in the fabrication of types of a very novel and difficult construction: while we find a Governor General, (unlike every description of public men in Britain) amidst all the busy scenes of war and state affairs, cultivating the arts of peace; advicing, soliciting, animating men of ability
to undertake, to persevere, and to accomplish pursuits so laudable in themselves, and so strongly pointed to attest and extend the India Company's most essential interests in Bengal.[16]

The review drew upon an easy equation between the study of Indian languages and its use in maintaining the British empire in India. The argument that was made was an interesting one: the aim of the British government was "to establish an empire over the minds as well as over the country of the natives," and grammar books were needed to allow for an "easy" intercourse with the "native" as no people could "cheerfully submit to rulers" they did not understand."[17] The central assumption within eighteenth century British print culture, where print technology was seen at the apex of communication forms, was transferred

---

[16] Ibid., p. 12. Print actually began in 'Hindostan' in 1556 when the Jesuits established the first printing press in Goa.

[17] Ibid., p. 5.

onto the colonies by the East India Company. Such was the realm of print that evolved in Calcutta in the last two decades of the twentieth century to serve the needs of the empire.

At the turn of the century, books made their way into Indian society and began to displace a manuscript culture. Natives started to read, make use of and negotiate their lives through printed texts. Moreover, the press initiated a shift in the very nature of how texts were to be written, preserved and disseminated. In fact, it initiated a shift in the very method of writing, a shift that involved cultural habits – Indians would sit on the floor and write, unlike Europeans who used tables and chairs. Nathaniel Halhed describes it in the following manner: "As they have neither chairs nor tables, their posture in writing is very different from ours: they sit upon their heels, or sometimes upon their hams, while their left hand held open serves as a desk whereon to lay the paper on which they write, which is kept in its place by the thumb: so that they never write on a large sheet of paper without folding it down to a very small surface"[18] It is fascinating to conjecture as to how exactly the change to print took place. As more and more natives had access to printed texts, that which had been the privilege of a particular class of people, now became democratized. Now, a large canvas of Indian society had access to printed books. How did it feel to be able to touch

---

[18] Nathaniel Halhed, *A Grammar of the Bengal Language*, p. 2.

printed paper and read, and be aware that many others across the land were also reading the same text? Indians closely interacted with the Britishers and learnt their social manners, learning how the technology worked. They also learnt the different uses that print could come into.

CHARACTERISTICS OF SCRIBAL CULTURE.

Scribal-manuscript culture was defined as archaic and not very reliable. Halhed represents these elements of inauthenticity as inherent in the behavioural habits of the natives, stating that it was with "obstinate and inviolable obscurity the Jentoos conceal ... the Mysteries of their faith."[19] This particular grammar text, like other books printed by the scholar-administrators of the East India Company, would undo by making public the concealment, "obscurity" and archaic-ness of scribal knowledge. Halhed was engaged in revealing the knowledge systems that were "shut up in the libraries of Brahmins,"[20] and in undoing the "impenetrable reserve" of the Hindus.[21]

SIR WILLIAM JONES.

Sir William Jones, is a perfect example of a scholar who worked outside the Orientalist knowledge-making

---

[19] Halhed, *A Grammar*, p. x.

[20] Ibid., p. iii.

[21] Ibid., p. xi.

framework. He was also steeped in the culture of
eighteenth century British print and had an immense trust
in the veracity of printed texts. An employee of the East
India Company, Jones examined Indian languages in order
to make linguistic connections with European languages,
drawing attention to the complexities of the local culture
while also placing it on a "pattern of human history at a
global level."[22] In his annual address to the Asiatic Society
in Calcutta, which he founded, in February 1789, Jones
described the Sanskrit language within a global context,
stating; that "the Sanskrit language, whatever be its
antiquity, is of a wonderful structure; [it is] more perfect
than the Greek, more copious than the Latin, and more
exquisitely refined than either, yet bearing to both of them
a stronger affinity."[23] Jones had a very clear idea of how the
Asiatic Society would operate, revealing an awareness that
the process of Company-sponsored Orientalist knowledge
construction would have to involve the natives. Jones
makes it clear when he says:

> Much may … be expected from the communications
> of learned natives, whether lawyers, physicians, or
> private scholars, who should eagerly, on the first
> invitation, send us their … [works] on a variety of

[22] Kapil Raj. "Refashioning Civilities, Engineering Trust: William Jones,
Indian Intermediaries and the Production of Reliable Legal Knowledge in
Late Eighteenth Century Bengal," *Studies in History* 17(2001): 23-47, 29.

[23] William Jones, *The Collected Works of Sir William Jones. 3 Vols.* (New York:
New York University Press, 1993), *Vol. 3*, p. 34.

subjects.... With a view to avail ourselves of this disposition, and to bring their latent science under our inspection, it might be advisable to print and circulate a short memorial, in Persian and Hindi ... [advertising] the design of our institution. ... To instruct others is the prescribed duty of learned Brahmans, and, if they be men of substance, without reward; ... and the Mahomedans have not only the permission, but the positive commands, of their law giver, to search for learning even in the remotest parts of the globe.[24]

In his address to the white diasporic community in Calcutta comprising scholar-administrators, Sir William Jones encourages them to be involved in the apparatuses of knowledge-gathering, laying out specific instructions as to how they were to work. They were to "contribute a succinct description of such manuscripts" as had been "perused or inspected, with their dates and the names of their owners, and to propose for solution such questions as had occurred to him concerning Asiatik Art, Science, and History, natural or civil"; subsequently, the Asiatic Society would "possess without labour, ... a fuller catalogue of Oriental books."[25] It was through a collaborative process, dependent on a relationship between the scholar and natives, that a catalogue of Oriental books could be

---

[24] Jones, *Collected Works, Vol. 3*, pp. 21-22.

[25] Ibid., pp. 21-22.

established. Jones was implementing the strictures of British eighteenth century print culture, evident in his valorization of print technology as against manuscript culture.

Manuscripts are seen as being less than perfect while printed texts allow for true, correct knowledge to emerge. Print technology is invested with a kind of truth power that is denied to manuscripts. Power resides in the capacity to be able to use print, and in the process, to make it accessible to larger groups of people. Mechanical reproducibility, made possible as a result of letterpress technology, would make knowledge more reproducible but also more authentic. The realm of print spread across continents, and made it possible to control the colonial territories.

EXTRACTS FROM THE ENGLISH PREFACES OF THE TRANSLATED TEXTS OF *MANUSMRITI*, WRITTEN UNDER THE PATRONAGE OF THE EAST INDIA COMPANY.

These extracts from the "Prefaces" draw attention to the methods that were used by the EIC sponsored Orientalist scholars in translating manuscript-texts from Indian languages into English. We can ask ourselves the following questions:

1. How did these Orientalist scholars locate the manuscripts?
2. Who assisted them in these translations?
3. Did they make use of numerous versions of the same manuscript-text?

3 INTRODUCTION BY THE REVD. P. PERCIVAL.[26]

The Professor of Hindu Literature in the East India College, Graves Chamney Haughton, M. A., F.R.S., in the year One Thousand Eight Hundred and Twenty five, published the original Sanskrit text of *Manava Dharma Séstra*, or the *Institutes of Manu*. His beautiful Edition was, by permission, dedicated to the reigning Sovereign of the time.

...

Although the Editor had to perform the task he took in hand under great disadvantages,——having no native Pundits to consult on the countless nice points of criticism with which he had to deal,——his talent and his rare acquirements enabled him to complete it with great and acknowledged success. His Edition of the original text,——

---

[26] *Manavadharmasastra, or, The Institutes of Manu,* according to the Gloss of Kulluka, comprising the Indian system of Duties, Religious and Civil. Verbally translated from the original, with a Preface by Sir William Jones, and Collated with the Sanskrit Text, by Graves Chanmey Haughton, Esq., Professor of Hindu Literature in the East India College. THIRD EDITION, edited by The Revd. P. Percival, Professor of Vernacular Literature, Presidency College, Madras. (Madras, J. Higginbotham: 1863).

the result of a careful comparison of nine manuscripts, obtained from various parts of India, with a printed copy executed by Babu Ram, a learned Pundit of Calcutta,—was enriched by critical and explanatory notes. By the unanimous voice of competent judges, Haughton's Edition of the text of Manu has ever been considered as, "one of the most beautiful monuments of true philological research combined with sound criticism that Hindu Literature has to boast of."

More than thirty years before the Edition abovementioned issued from the press, Sir William Jones, justly celebrated for his profound and varied acquirements in different departments of learning, and, more particularly by reason of his great attainments in Oriental Literature, had directed his attention to the Code of Manu. He regarded it as one of the most important records of Hindu antiquity, and therefore resolved, if possible, to prepare an English version for the information of his countrymen. In the attempt to gain an adequate acquaintance with the ancient and sacred Shastra, he had to encounter obstacles almost insuperable. Bigotry and superstition alike opposed him, notwithstanding his high official position. At Benares, the Chief Native Magistrate was unsuccessful in his attempts to procure a Persian translation of the work, the Pundits being unanimous in their refusal to render assistance. The Pundit, with whom Sir William read Sanskrit, reluctantly consented to lend his aid, but only on certain days, when planetary influences were favorable. As preparations for the publication of an English version advanced, the Pundit became alarmed at the prospect of Sir William's success, and apprehending serious consequences to himself, he earnestly requested that his name might in no way appear in connection with the attempt to make known to foreigners the sacred Institutes of the revered Hindu legislator. Eventually a wealthy Hindu at Gaya, caused a version to be made, which assisted Sir William in his design, and enabled him, at an enormous expense of time and labor, to give the result of his endeavours to the European world in an English version. The translation appeared in the, year 1792.

Knowing that the Code was revered by the Hindus as a divine revelation, and universally accepted by them as an unerring guide and directory in all things civil and religious, and consequently the basis on which National Institutions rested, the Government of India ordered an Edition of Sir William's translation to be printed in Calcutta, in a form convenient for reference: it came out of the press in the year 1794.

4 PREFATORY NOTE BY SIR WILLIAM JONES (1794).[27]

PREFACE

BY

SIR WILLIAM JONES

The name of MANU is clearly derived (like *menees*, *mens*, and *mind*) from the root *men to understand* ; and it signifies, as all the Pundits agree, *intelligent*, particularly in the doctrines of the *Veda*, which the composer of our *Dharma Sa'stra* must have studied very diligently; since great numbers of its texts, changed only in a few syllables for the sake of the measure, are interspersed through the work and cited at length in the commentaries: the Public may, therefore,

---

[27] Ibid.

assure themselves, that they now possess a considerable part of the Hindu scripture, without the dullness of its profane ritual or much of its mystical jargon, DA'RA SHUCU'H was persuaded, and not without sound reason, that the first MANU of the Brahmans could be no other person than the progenitor of mankind, to whom *Jews, Christians,* and *Musulmans* unite in giving the name of ADAM; but, whoever he might have been, he is highly honoured by name in the Veda itself, where it is declared, that whatever MANU pronounced, was a medicine for the soul; and the sage VRIHASPATI, now supposed to preside over the planet Jupiter, says in his own law tract, that "MANU held the first rank among legislators, because he had expressed in his code the whole sense of the *Veda*; that no code was approved, which contradicted MANU; that other *Shastras*, and treatises on grammar or logic, retained splendour so long only, as MANU, who taught the way to just wealth, to virtue, and to final happiness, was not seen in competition with them;" VYASA too, the son of PARA'SARA before mentioned, has decided, that the Veda with its *Angas*, or the six compositions deduced from it, the revealed system of medicine, the *Puranas*, or sacred histories, and the code of MANU, were four works of supreme authority, which ought never to be shaken by arguments merely human.

...

A number of glosses or comments on MANU were composed by the *Munis*, or old philosophers, whose treatises, together with that before us, constitute the

Dharma Shastra, in a collective sense, or Body of Law; among the more modern commentaries, that called *Medhatithi*, that by GO'VINDARA'JA, and that by DHARANI'-DHARA, were once in the greatest repute; but the first was reckoned prolix and unequal; the second, concise but obscure; and the third, often erroneous. At length appeared KULLU'KA BHATTA; who, after a painful course of study and the collation of numerous manuscripts, produced a work, of which it may, perhaps, be said very truly, that it is the shortest, yet the most luminous, the least ostentatious, yet the most learned, the deepest, yet the most agreeable, commentary ever composed on any author ancient or modern, European or Asiatic. The Pandits care so little for genuine chronology, that none of them can tell me the age of KULLU'KA, whom they always name with applause; but he informs us himself, that he was a *Brahmin* of the *Varéndra* tribe, whose family had been long settled in *Gaur* or Bengal, but that he had chosen his residence among the learned on the banks of the holy river at Ka'si. His text and interpretation I have almost implicitly followed, though I had myself collated many copies of MANU, and among them a manuscript of a very ancient date: his gloss is here printed in *Italics;* and any reader, who may choose to pass it over as if unprinted, will have in *Roman* letters an exact version of the original, and may form some idea of its character and structure, as well as of the *Sanskrit* idiom, which must necessarily be preserved in a verbal translation; and a translation, not scrupulously verbal, would have been highly improper in a work on so delicate and momentous a subject as private and criminal jurisprudence

Should a series of Brahmans omit, for three generations, the reading of MANU, their sacerdotal class, as all the Pandits assure me, would in strictness be forfeited; but they must explain it only to their pupils of the three highest classes; and the Brahman who read it with me, requested most earnestly, that his name might be concealed; nor would he have read it for any consideration on a forbidden day of the moon, or without the ceremonies prescribed in the second and fourth chapters for a lecture on the Veda: so great, indeed, is the idea of sanctity annexed to this book, that, when the chief native magistrate at Benares endeavoured, at my request, to procure a Persian translation of it, before I had a hope of being at any time able to understand the original, the Pandits of his court unanimously and positively refused to assist in the work; nor should I have procured it at all, if a wealthy Hindu at Gaya had not caused the version to be made by some of his dependants, at the desire of my friend Mr. LAW. The Persian translation of MANU, like all others from the Sanskrit into that language, is a rude intermixture of the text, loosely rendered, with some old or new comment, and often with the crude notions of the translator; and, though it expresses the general sense of the original, yet it swarms with errors, imputable partly to haste, and partly to ignorance: thus where MANU says, *that emissaries are the eyes of a prince*, the Persian phrase makes him ascribe four eyes to the person of a king; for the word *char*, which means *an emissary in Sanskrit*, signifies *four* in the popular dialect.

PARTS FROM THE *MANAVADHARMA* THAT SHOULD BE ERASED AS THEY ARE OBJECTIONABLE.

5 OBJECTIONABLE EXTRACTS FROM THE *MANAVADHARMA*

CHAPTERS 2 AND 3

Chapter 2.

67. The nuptial ceremony is stated to be the Vedic sacrament for women (and to be equal to the initiation), serving the husband (equivalent to) the residence in (the house of the) teacher, and the household duties (the same) as the (daily) worship of the sacred fire.

Chapter 3.

2. (A student) who has studied in due order the three Vedas, or two, or even one only, without breaking the (rules of) studentship, shall enter the order of householders.

3. He who is famous for (the strict performance of) his duties and has received his heritage, the Veda, from his father, shall be honoured, sitting on a couch and adorned with a garland, with (the present of) a cow (and the honey-mixture).

4. Having bathed, with the permission of his teacher, and performed according to the rule the Samavartana (the rite on returning home), a twice-born man shall marry a wife of equal caste who is endowed with auspicious (bodily) marks.

5. A damsel who is neither a Sapinda on the mother's side, nor belongs to the same family on the father's side, is recommended to twice-born men for wedlock and conjugal union.

6. In connecting himself with a wife, let him carefully avoid the ten following families, be they ever so great, or rich in kine, horses, sheep, grain, or (other) property,

7. (Viz.) one which neglects the sacred rites, one in which no male children (are born), one in which the Veda is not studied, one (the members of) which have thick hair on the body, those which are subject to hemorrhoids, phthisis, weakness of digestion, epilepsy, or white or black leprosy.

8. Let him not marry a maiden (with) reddish (hair), nor one who has a redundant member, nor one who is sickly, nor one either with no hair (on the body) or too much, nor one who is garrulous or has red (eyes),

9. Nor one named after a constellation, a tree, or a river, nor one bearing the name of a low caste, or of a mountain, nor one named after a bird, a snake, or a slave, nor one whose name inspires terror.

10. Let him wed a female free from bodily defects, who has an agreeable name, the (graceful) gait of a Hamsa or of an elephant, a moderate (quantity of) hair on the body and on the head, small teeth, and soft limbs.

11. But a prudent man should not marry (a maiden) who has no brother, nor one whose father is not known, through fear lest (in the former case she be made) an appointed daughter (and in the latter) lest (he should commit) sin.

12. For the first marriage of twice-born men (wives) of equal caste are recommended; but for those who through desire proceed (to marry again) the following females, (chosen) according to the (direct) order (of the castes), are most approved.

13. It is declared that a Sudra woman alone (can be) the wife of a Sudra, she and one of his own caste (the wives) of a Vaisya, those two and one of his own caste (the wives) of a Kshatriya, those three and one of his own caste (the wives) of a Brahmana.

14. A Sudra woman is not mentioned even in any (ancient) story as the (first) wife of a Brahmana or of a Kshatriya, though they lived in the (greatest) distress.

15. Twice-born men who, in their folly, wed wives of the low (Sudra) caste, soon degrade their families and their children to the state of Sudras.

16. According to Atri and to (Gautama) the son of Utathya, he who weds a Sudra woman becomes an outcast, according to Saunaka on the birth of a son, and according to Bhrigu he who has (male) offspring from a (Sudra female, alone).

17. A Brahmana who takes a Sudra wife to his bed, will (after death) sink into hell; if he begets a child by her, he will lose the rank of a Brahmana.

18. The manes and the gods will not eat the (offerings) of that man who performs the rites in honour of the gods, of the manes, and of guests chiefly with a (Sudra wife's) assistance, and such (a man) will not go to heaven.

19. For him who drinks the moisture of a Sudra's lips, who is tainted by her breath, and who begets a son on her, no expiation is prescribed.

20. Now listen to (the) brief (description of) the following eight marriage-rites used by the four castes (varna) which partly secure benefits and partly produce evil both in this life and after death.

21. (They are) the rite of Brahman (Brahma), that of the gods (Daiva), that of the Rishis (Arsha), that of Pragapati (Pragapatya), that of the Asuras (Asura), that of the Gandharvas (Gandharva), that of the Rhashasas (Rakshasa), and that of the Pisakas (Paisaka).

22. Which is lawful for each caste (varna) and which are the virtues or faults of each (rite), all this I will declare to you, as well as their good and evil results with respect to the offspring.

23. One may know that the first six according to the order (followed above) are lawful for a Brahmana, the four last for a Kshatriya, and the same four, excepting the Rakshasa rite, for a Vaisya and a Sudra.

24. The sages state that the first four are approved (in the case) of a Brahmana, one, the Rakshasa (rite in the case) of a Kshatriya, and the Asura (marriage in that) of a Vaisya and of a Sudra.

25. But in these (Institutes of the sacred law) three of the five (last) are declared to be lawful and two unlawful; the Paisaka and the Asura (rites) must never be used.

26. For Kshatriyas those before-mentioned two rites, the Gandharva and the Rakshasa, whether separate or mixed, are permitted by the sacred tradition.

27. The gift of a daughter, after decking her (with costly garments) and honouring (her by presents of jewels), to a man learned in the Veda and of good conduct, whom (the father) himself invites, is called the Brahma rite.

28. The gift of a daughter who has been decked with ornaments, to a priest who duly officiates at a sacrifice, during the course of its performance, they call the Daiva rite.

29. When (the father) gives away his daughter according to the rule, after receiving from the bridegroom, for (the fulfilment of) the sacred law, a cow and a bull or two pairs, that is named the Arsha rite.

30. The gift of a daughter (by her father) after he has addressed (the couple) with the text, 'May both of you perform together your duties,' and has shown honour (to the bridegroom), is called in the Smriti the Pragapatya rite.

31. When (the bridegroom) receives a maiden, after having given as much wealth as he can afford, to the kinsmen and to the bride herself, according to his own will, that is called the Asura rite.

32. The voluntary union of a maiden and her lover one must know (to be) the Gandharva rite, which springs from desire and has sexual intercourse for its purpose.

33. The forcible abduction of a maiden from her home, while she cries out and weeps, after (her kinsmen) have been slain or wounded and (their houses) broken open, is called the Rakshasa rite.

34. When (a man) by stealth seduces a girl who is sleeping, intoxicated, or disordered in intellect, that is the eighth, the most base and sinful rite of the Pisakas.

35. The gift of daughters among Brahmanas is most approved, (if it is preceded) by (a libation of) water; but in the case of other castes (it may be performed) by (the expression of) mutual consent.

36. Listen now to me, ye Brahmanas, while I fully declare what quality has been ascribed by Manu to each of these marriage-rites.

37. The son of a wife wedded according to the Brahma rite, if he performs meritorious acts, liberates from sin ten ancestors, ten descendants and himself as the twenty-first.

38. The son born of a wife, wedded according to the Daiva rite, likewise (saves) seven ancestors and seven descendants, the son of a wife married by the Arsha rite

49

three (in the ascending and descending lines), and the son of a wife married by the rite of Ka (Pragapati) six (in either line).

39. From the four marriages, (enumerated) successively, which begin with the Brahma rite spring sons, radiant with knowledge of the Veda and honoured by the Sishtas (good men).

40. Endowed with the qualities of beauty and goodness, possessing wealth and fame, obtaining as many enjoyments as they desire and being most righteous, they will live a hundred years.

41. But from the remaining (four) blamable marriages spring sons who are cruel and speakers of untruth, who hate the Veda and the sacred law.

42. In the blameless marriages blameless children are born to men, in blamable (marriages) blamable (offspring); one should therefore avoid the blamable (forms of marriage).

43. The ceremony of joining the hands is prescribed for (marriages with) women of equal caste (varna); know that the following rule (applies) to weddings with females of a different caste (varna).

44. On marrying a man of a higher caste a Kshatriya bride must take hold of an arrow, a Vaisya bride of a goad, and a Sudra female of the hem of the (bridegroom's) garment.

45. Let (the husband) approach his wife in due season, being constantly satisfied with her (alone); he may also,

being intent on pleasing her, approach her with a desire for conjugal union (on any day) excepting the Parvans.

46. Sixteen (days and) nights (in each month), including four days which differ from the rest and are censured by the virtuous, (are called) the natural season of women.

47. But among these the first four, the eleventh and the thirteenth are (declared to be) forbidden; the remaining nights are recommended.

48. On the even nights sons are conceived and daughters on the uneven ones; hence a man who desires to have sons should approach his wife in due season on the even (nights).

49. A male child is produced by a greater quantity of male seed, a female child by the prevalence of the female; if (both are) equal, a hermaphrodite or a boy and a girl; if (both are) weak or deficient in quantity, a failure of conception (results).

50. He who avoids women on the six forbidden nights and on eight others, is (equal in chastity to) a student, in whichever order he may live.

51. No father who knows (the law) must take even the smallest gratuity for his daughter; for a man who, through avarice, takes a gratuity, is a seller of his offspring.

52. But those (male) relations who, in their folly, live on the separate property of women, (e.g. appropriate) the beasts of burden, carriages, and clothes of women, commit sin and will sink into hell.

53. Some call the cow and the bull (given) at an Arsha wedding 'a gratuity;' (but) that is wrong, since (the acceptance of) a fee, be it small or great, is a sale (of the daughter).

54. When the relatives do not appropriate (for their use) the gratuity (given), it is not a sale; (in that case) the (gift) is only a token of respect and of kindness towards the maidens.

55. Women must be honoured and adorned by their fathers, brothers, husbands, and brothers-in-law, who desire (their own) welfare.

56. Where women are honoured, there the gods are pleased; but where they are not honoured, no sacred rite yields rewards.

57. Where the female relations live in grief, the family soon wholly perishes; but that family where they are not unhappy ever prospers.

58. The houses on which female relations, not being duly honoured, pronounce a curse, perish completely, as if destroyed by magic.

59. Hence men who seek (their own) welfare, should always honour women on holidays and festivals with (gifts of) ornaments, clothes, and (dainty) food.

60. In that family, where the husband is pleased with his wife and the wife with her husband, happiness will assuredly be lasting.

61. For if the wife is not radiant with beauty, she will not attract her husband; but if she has no attractions for him, no children will be born.

62. If the wife is radiant with beauty, the whole house is bright; but if she is destitute of beauty, all will appear dismal.

63. By low marriages, by omitting (the performance of) sacred rites, by neglecting the study of the Veda, and by irreverence towards Brahmanas, (great) families sink low.

64. By (practising) handicrafts, by pecuniary transactions, by (begetting) children on Sudra females only, by (trading in) cows, horses, and carriages, by (the pursuit of) agriculture and by taking service under a king,

65. By sacrificing for men unworthy to offer sacrifices and by denying (the future rewards for good) works, families, deficient in the (knowledge of the) Veda, quickly perish.

66. But families that are rich in the knowledge of the Veda, though possessing little wealth, are numbered among the great, and acquire great fame.

67. With the sacred fire, kindled at the wedding, a householder shall perform according to the law the domestic ceremonies and the five (great) sacrifices, and (with that) he shall daily cook his food.

68. A householder has five slaughter-houses (as it were, viz.) the hearth, the grinding-stone, the broom, the pestle and mortar, the water-vessel, by using which he is bound (with the fetters of sin).

69. In order to successively expiate (the offences committed by means) of all these (five) the great sages have prescribed for householders the daily (performance of the five) great sacrifices.

70. Teaching (and studying) is the sacrifice (offered) to Brahman, the (offerings of water and food called) Tarpana the sacrifice to the manes, the burnt oblation the sacrifice offered to the gods, the Bali offering that offered to the Bhutas, and the hospitable reception of guests the offering to men.

71. He who neglects not these five great sacrifices, while he is able (to perform them), is not tainted by the sins (committed) in the five places of slaughter, though he constantly lives in the (order of) house (-holders).

72. But he who does not feed these five, the gods, his guests, those whom he is bound to maintain, the manes, and himself, lives not, though he breathes.

73. They call (these) five sacrifices also, Ahuta, Huta, Prahuta, Brahmya-huta, and Prasita.

74. Ahuta (not offered in the fire) is the muttering (of Vedic texts), Huta the burnt oblation (offered to the gods), Prahuta (offered by scattering it on the ground) the Bali offering given to the Bhutas, Brahmya-huta (offered in the digestive fire of Brahmanas), the respectful reception of Brahmana (guests), and Prasita (eaten) the (daily oblation to the manes, called) Tarpana.

75. Let (every man) in this (second order, at least) daily apply himself to the private recitation of the Veda, and also

to the performance of the offering to the gods; for he who is diligent in the performance of sacrifices, supports both the movable and the immovable creation.

76. An oblation duly thrown into the fire, reaches the sun; from the sun comes rain, from rain food, therefrom the living creatures (derive their subsistence).

77. As all living creatures subsist by receiving support from air, even so (the members of) all orders subsist by receiving support from the householder.

78. Because men of the three (other) orders are daily supported by the householder with (gifts of) sacred knowledge and food, therefore (the order of) householders is the most excellent order.

150. Manu has declared that those Brahmanas who are thieves, outcasts, eunuchs, or atheists are unworthy (to partake) of oblations to the gods and manes.

151. Let him not entertain at a Sraddha one who wears his hair in braids (a student), one who has not studied (the Veda), one afflicted with a skin-disease, a gambler, nor those who sacrifice for a multitude (of sacrificers).

152. Physicians, temple-priests, sellers of meat, and those who subsist by shop-keeping must be avoided at sacrifices offered to the gods and to the manes.

153. A paid servant of a village or of a king, man with deformed nails or black teeth, one who opposes his teacher, one who has forsaken the sacred fire, and a usurer;

154. One suffering from consumption, one who subsists by tending cattle, a younger brother who marries or kindles the sacred fire before the elder, one who neglects the five great sacrifices, an enemy of the Brahmana race, an elder brother who marries or kindles the sacred fire after the younger, and one who belongs to a company or corporation,

155. An actor or singer, one who has broken the vow of studentship, one whose (only or first) wife is a Sudra female, the son of a remarried woman, a one-eyed man, and he in whose house a paramour of his wife (resides);

156. He who teaches for a stipulated fee and he who is taught on that condition, he who instructs Sudra pupils and he whose teacher is a Sudra, he who speaks rudely, the son of an adulteress, and the son of a widow,

157. He who forsakes his mother, his father, or a teacher without a (sufficient) reason, he who has contracted an alliance with outcasts either through the Veda or through a marriage,

158. An incendiary, a prisoner, he who eats the food given by the son of an adulteress, a seller of Soma, he who undertakes voyages by sea, a bard, an oil-man, a suborner to perjury,

159. He who wrangles or goes to law with his father, the keeper of a gambling-house, a drunkard, he who is afflicted with a disease (in punishment of former) crimes, he who is accused of a mortal sin, a hypocrite, a seller of substances used for flavouring food,

160. A maker of bows and of arrows, he who lasciviously dallies with a brother's widow, the betrayer of a friend, one who subsists by gambling, he who learns (the Veda) from his son,

CHAPTER 4

35. Keeping his hair, nails, and beard clipped, subduing his passions by austerities, wearing white garments and (keeping himself) pure, he shall be always engaged in studying the Veda and (such acts as are) conducive to his welfare.

36. He shall carry a staff of bamboo, a pot full of water, a sacred string, a bundle of Kusa grass, and (wear) two bright golden ear-rings.

37. Let him never look at the sun, when he sets or rises, is eclipsed or reflected in water, or stands in the middle of the sky.

38. Let him not step over a rope to which a calf is tied, let him not run when it rains, and let him not look at his own image in water; that is a settled rule.

39. Let him pass by (a mound of) earth, a cow, an idol, a Brahmana, clarified butter, honey, a crossway, and well-known trees, turning his right hand towards them.

40. Let him, though mad with desire, not approach his wife when her courses appear; nor let him sleep with her in the same bed.

41. For the wisdom, the energy, the strength, the sight, and the vitality of a man who approaches a woman covered with menstrual excretions, utterly perish.

42. If he avoids her, while she is in that condition, his wisdom, energy, strength, sight, and vitality will increase.

43. Let him not eat in the company of his wife, nor look at her, while she eats, sneezes, yawns, or sits at her ease.

44. A Brahmana who desires energy must not look at (a woman) who applies collyrium to her eyes, has anointed or uncovered herself or brings forth (a child).

45. Let him not eat, dressed with one garment only; let him not bathe naked; let him not void urine on a road, on ashes, or in a cow-pen,

46. Nor on ploughed land, in water, on an altar of bricks, on a mountain, on the ruins of a temple, nor ever on an ant-hill,

47. Nor in holes inhabited by living creatures, nor while he walks or stands, nor on reaching the bank of a river, nor on the top of a mountain.

48. Let him never void faeces or urine, facing the wind, or a fire, or looking towards a Brahmana, the sun, water, or cows.

49. He may ease himself, having covered (the ground) with sticks, clods, leaves, grass, and the like, restraining his speech, (keeping himself) pure, wrapping up his body, and covering his head.

50. Let him void faeces and urine, in the daytime turning to the north, at night turning towards the south, during the two twilights in the same (position) as by day.

51. In the shade or in darkness a Brahmana may, both by day and at night, do it, assuming any position he pleases; likewise when his life is in danger.

52. The intellect of (a man) who voids urine against a fire, the sun, the moon, in water, against a Brahmana, a cow, or the wind, perishes.

53. Let him not blow a fire with his mouth; let him not look at a naked woman; let him not throw any impure substance into the fire, and let him not warm his feet at it.

54. Let him not place (fire) under (a bed or the like); nor step over it, nor place it (when he sleeps) at the foot-(end of his bed); let him not torment living creatures.

55. Let him not eat, nor travel, nor sleep during the twilight; let him not scratch the ground; let him not take off his garland.

NOTES:

This text is a collaboration with:
O₂pen Windows: A Feminist Resource and Research Center.

O₂pen Windows is a feminist research cum *adda* center, based in Bangalore, India. If it could, it would sustain itself with endless cups of tea and lots of stimulating research.

The Purpose: We hope to open up the realm of religious discourse into the public domain of the secular; if we – the people – take these texts into our hands – then, we can do away with those parts that are misogynous and caste-ist and are fundamentally unconstitutional. We, the citizens, need to petition to the government to ensure that religious institutions comply with the laws of the land, and as India is a signatory to CEDAW – the nation complies with it and does not allow any institution (religious or otherwise) to violate it.